SOPHIA'S BROKEN CRAYONS

Crystal Falk

Edited by Kathea Smith

 Forward by Jon Anderson, Surrogacy Together

Sophia's Broken Crayons

https://www.facebook.com/pages/Sophias-Broken-Crayons/623367251089433
Birth, Bump and Beyond, LLC. First Edition

For Katelyn and Luther

A Special Thanks from the Author to

Surrogacy Together
All Things Surrogacy
Square Foot Gardening 4 U
Kim Roman
Amanda Schaeffer

Forward by
Surrogacy Together

It is an incredible feeling when someone can brighten your life and add color to a place that once seemed so dark. "Sophia's Broken Crayons" is a story that represents, with simplicity, the selflessness of others. I get to experience that benevolence everyday, because a very good friend and her family gave my wife and I the best gift possible. Our daughter was born in 2010 through surrogacy. We celebrate surrogacy everyday; with every hug, every kiss and every "hold me daddy." She will grow up and learn about the special people that helped bring her into our life and how it brought so much happiness.

After having two of her own children, the author Crystal Falk, witnessed the heartbreak and pain of infertility as she watched one of her closest friends struggle with having a baby. Falk became a surrogate for her friend. She decided to write "Sophia's Broken Crayons" about her own experience in words her two- year old daughter would understand. Her daughter loved the story and grasped the concept of why someone would choose to help a friend though surrogacy. This book is an inspiring example of how at even a young age one can understand the power of giving to others.

In life, no matter where you are, or what you do, at some point we may need to reach out for help. Somewhere along the line are people who step up to the plate for you, believe in you, and stand by you. As the Executive Director of Surrogacy Together it is rewarding to be part of these incredible journeys and see how surrogacy not only brought me happiness but also to so many other families.

Jon Anderson
Executive Director of Surrogacy Together

THE FERTILITY LAW FIRM

KUMAR FAMILY
FOUNDATION

Surrogacy
Together

A little girl named Sophia lived in a pretty house...

with her mommy, daddy, and little brother Bobby.

Sophia loved her mommy and daddy very much.
And she loved her brother too, most of the time.

She loved to color with her crayons and make pretty pictures,

but sometimes Bobby would break her crayons

and that would make Sophia sad.

Sophia had very good friends. When she was sad,
her friends would share their crayons with her.

This made Sophia very happy.

Sophia's mommy and daddy had very good friends too.
Their names were Mr. and Mrs. Johnson.

They always wanted to have a baby but Mrs. Johnson's belly was broken. This made them very sad.

Although Mrs. Johnson's belly was broken and couldn't carry a baby, Sophia's mommy's worked just fine.

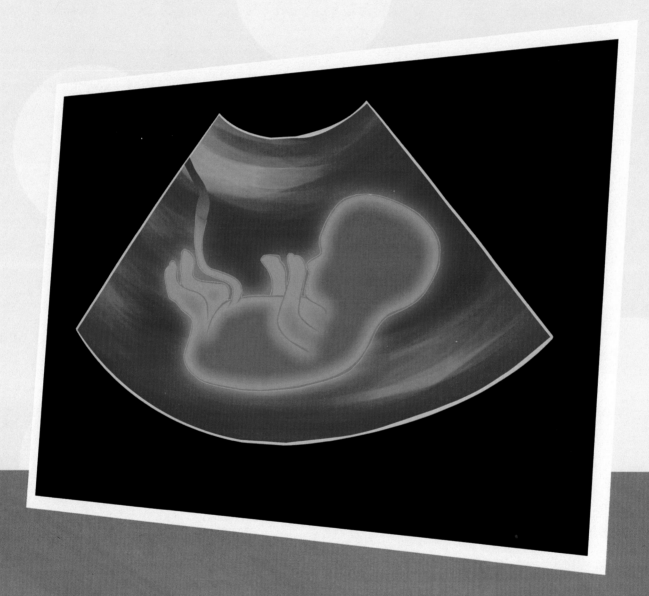

Because they were such very good friends,
Sophia's mom let them use her belly to grow a baby.

Mr. and Mrs. Johnson were so happy and thankful to their friends.

"We're having a baby!" Mr. and Mrs. Johnson told everyone with joy.

Everyone was excited to know they were having a baby.

Bigger and bigger, Sophia's mommy's belly grew as the days went by.

The Johnson's friends and family gave them presents for their new baby.

One day, Mr. and Mrs. Johnson's baby was ready to come out of Sophia's mom's belly. Everyone was very excited to see the new baby.

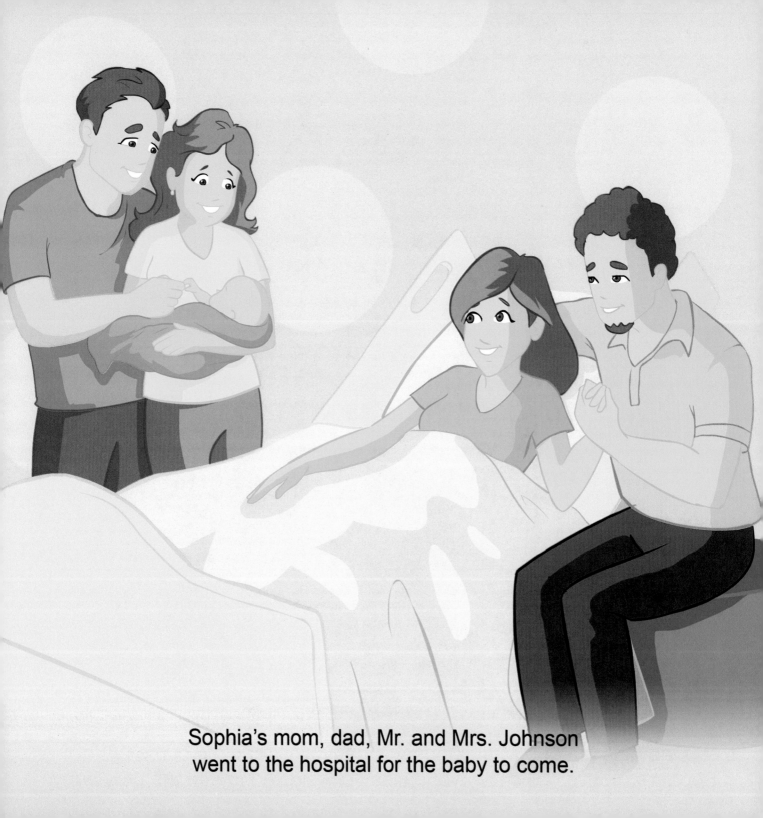

Sophia's mom, dad, Mr. and Mrs. Johnson
went to the hospital for the baby to come.

The Johnson's were very happy to see and hold their baby for the first time.

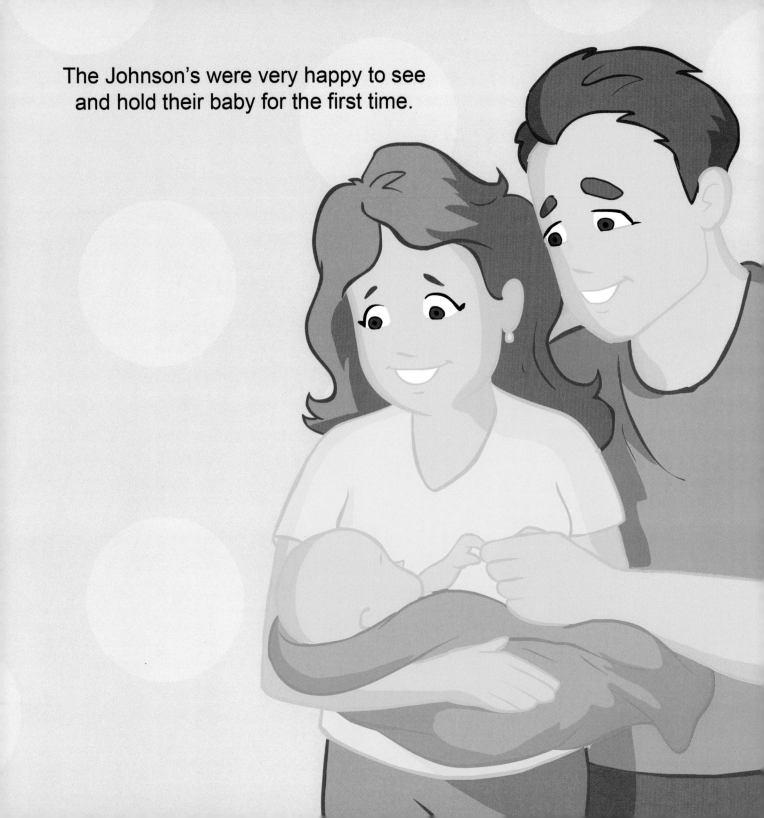

Sophia's parents were very happy also.
Mr. and Mrs. Johnson were not sad anymore,

just like Sophia's friends made her feel
when they shared their crayons.

A beautiful gift was given to make the sadness go away

and to make the world a happier place. All it took was a heart that wanted to share happiness.

SURROGACY TOGETHER FRIENDS ASSOCIATION

We would like to express our gratitude to all those who have already helped create families through Surrogacy. We admire the vision, the creativity, and the independent spirit of the original Intended Parents and Surrogates, as well as those just joining our Community that continue to step up each day to be part of a Miracle.

Every day we have the opportunity to hear stories from people whose lives have been altered for the better by their experience as a member of the Surrogacy Community.

These individuals have made a steadfast commitment to our community and we hope that you join us with pride while we recognize the amazing Surrogates, Intended Parents and the supporting friends and family that make our community remarkable. They have made the world a happier place and we are proud to call them our friends.

SURROGATES

1994
Susan Wilson 94 ♥, 97 ♥, 01 ♥
1995
Julie Tate 95 ♥, 97 ♥, 99 ♥/♥
1996
Michele Subia 96 ♥, 03 ♥, 06 ♥, 07 ♥, 09 ♥
1998
Jennifer Shores 98, 06, 07, 09
2000
Cathleen Boegel 00 ♥/♥, 02 ♥/♥, 05 ♥/♥, 08 ♥/♥
2001
Toni Anderson 01 ♥, 08 ♥, 12 ♥/♥
2002
Christina Bedway-Sipe 02 ♥, 04 ♥/♥
Erin Pope 02 ♥/♥, 04 ♥, 07 ♥
Susan Irvine 02 ♥, 07 ♥, 08 ♥
2003
Kerri Mullins 03 ♥, 04 ♥, 08 ♥
Stacie Grebner 03 ♥/♥/♥, 08 ♥/♥, 09 ♥, 12 ♥, 13 ♥
2004
Chasity Beaver 04 ♥, 08 ♥/♥, 09 ♥/♥
Chielo Baker 04 ♥, 05 ♥, 06 ♥/♥, 09 ♥/♥, 10 ♥
Jennifer Tipton-Arnold 04 ♥, 06 ♥
2005
Amy Booker 05 ♥/♥, 07 ♥, 13 ♥
Bonnie Downing 05 ♥, 08 ♥, 11 ♥, 14 ♥
Jenn Alcala 05 ♥, 11 ♥
Kat Kirkbride 05 ♥/♥, 07 ♥/♥, 09 ♥/♥
2006
Amie Lessard 06 ♥/♥, 08 ♥, 12 ♥
Chavonia Selock 06 ♥, 08 ♥, 09 ♥, 11 ♥, 14 ♥

Cynthia Begley 06 ♥/♥, 09 ♥/♥
Jill Reeder 06 ♥, 09 ♥/♥
Karen Poston 06 ♥, 08 ♥
Kathy Powers 06 ♥, 08 ♥, 10 ♥, 12 ♥/♥/♥
LaDonna Woodmansee 06 ♥, 09 ♥/♥, 11 ♥
Mary Carter 06, 08, 11
Signe Renteria 06 ♥, 08 ♥/♥
Susan Bitner 06 ♥/♥, 08 ♥/♥, 10 ♥, 13 ♥
2007
Adrienne Black 07 ♥, 09 ♥/♥, 12 ♥/♥
Amber Patterson 07 ♥, 08 ♥
Amanda Sager 07 ♥/♥, 12 ♥, 14 ♥
Bethany Jones 07, 12
Christine Gilbert 07 ♥/♥, 08 ♥, 13 ♥
Christina Thursby 07 ♥, 08 ♥/♥, 12 ♥, 13 ♥/♥
Erica Cordova Uphoff 07 ♥/♥, 08 ♥, 10 ♥/♥, 12 ♥
Gina Farley 07 ♥, 12 ♥
Jennifer Sokolowski-Kelly 07 ♥, 09 ♥, 12 ♥, 13 ♥/♥
Jennifer Taylor 07 ♥/♥/♥, 08 ♥, 12 ♥
Julie Stern 07 ♥, 10 ♥, 11 ♥/♥, 13 ♥
Kari Jewell 07 ♥/♥, 09 ♥
Kari Lopez 07 ♥/♥, 09 ♥, 14 ♥/♥
Rebekah Hills 07 ♥, 10 ♥, 12 ♥/♥
Wendy Bartlett 07 ♥, 08 ♥
2008
Christie Neumann 08 ♥, 10 ♥
Dawn Keller 08 ♥
Heidi Meeker 08, 09
Kristie Biggs 08 ♥
Kristin Moore 08 ♥, 09 ♥/♥, 11 ♥/♥
Jessica Daniels 08 ♥/♥, 09 ♥, 14
Lena Corrado 08, 12
Lisa Jones 08 ♥, 09 ♥/♥, 12 ♥, 14 ♥/♥

♥ = Girls	♥ = Singleton	♥♥♥ = Triplets
♥ = Boys	♥♥ = Twins	## = Year surrogate baby was born

Nisha Myers 08 ♥/♥, 11 ♥/♥
Richelle Foss 08 ♥/♥, 11 ♥, 13 ♥
Robin Putscher 08 ♥, 09 ♥/♥/♥
Tammi Jensen 08 ♥/♥
Tina Galletti 08 ♥, 09 ♥/♥, 11 ♥/♥
Traci Woolard 08 ♥, 10 ♥, 12 ♥/♥
Trisha Lund 08 ♥, 11 ♥, 12 ♥/♥, 14
Yessica Maher 08 ♥, 10 ♥, 12 ♥/♥

2009
April Batdorf 09 ♥/♥
Candice Sandusky 09 ♥
Deanna Kulesar 09 ♥
Elizabeth Borgen 09
Elle Pomeroy 09 ♥/♥
Heather Rodriguez 09 ♥, 10 ♥, 13 ♥/♥
Heidi Day 09 ♥/♥, 11 ♥/♥
Jennifer Kamphaus 09 ♥
Jodi Gerber 09 ♥, 10 ♥, 13 ♥
Megan Hall 09 ♥, 11 ♥, 13 ♥
Nicole Fulwood 09 ♥
Nicole McGehee 09 ♥/♥, 11 ♥, 13 ♥
Rachele Bartlett 09 ♥, 10 ♥

2010
Angela Simpson 10 ♥/♥
Carolee Legard 10 ♥, 13 ♥/♥
Cathryn Ferrell 10 ♥/♥, 13 ♥/♥
Christina Spicer 10, 12
Dana Matthews 10 ♥, 12 ♥/♥
Didi Hamby-Perry 10 ♥, 12 ♥, 13 ♥
Emily Howard 10 ♥, 13 ♥, 14 ♥
Heather Symonds 10 ♥/♥, 12 ♥/♥
Holly Braasch 10 ♥, 12 ♥/♥
Ivy Meyers 10 ♥, 13 ♥
Jeannine Theriault 10 ♥/♥, 12 ♥
Jennifer Hoeflinger 10 ♥/♥
Jennifer Scott-Hitchcock 10 ♥, 11 ♥/♥, 13 ♥
Jodi Clemens 10 ♥/♥
Jody Dye 10 ♥, 13 ♥/♥
Kasey Vance 10 ♥, 13 ♥/♥
Kendra Baker 10 ♥, 12 ♥, 14 ♥
Kim Chapman 10 ♥, 12 ♥
Kimberly Eaker 10 ♥/♥, 14 ♥/♥
Kristen Foote 10 ♥/♥
Kristle Menozi 10 ♥, 13 ♥
Lena Trammell 10 ♥, 11 ♥/♥, 13 ♥, 14 ♥/♥
Nadine Willoughby 10 ♥, 13 ♥
Nicole Patrick 10

Paulina Lugo 10 ♥, 11 ♥/♥
Sarah Perito 10 ♥, 14 ♥
Simi Denson 10 ♥, 13 ♥/♥/♥
Tammi Mason 10 ♥/♥, 12 ♥/♥
Tiffany Main 10 ♥, 12 ♥/♥

2011
Amber Sierra 11 ♥/♥, 12 ♥
Amy Donahue 11 ♥
Bethany Torres 11 ♥/♥, 13 ♥/♥
Carmela Cancino 11 ♥, 14 ♥
Daisy Mathison 11 ♥/♥
Darshan Andrews 11 ♥, 14
Emily Lamar 11 ♥/♥, 14 ♥
Jamie Garrigan-Girton 11 ♥/♥, 13 ♥
Joanne Graham 11 ♥/♥
Krystle Wallace 11 ♥, 14 ♥
Laura Wheeler 11 ♥/♥, 13 ♥/♥
Lynn Puzzo 11 ♥, 13 ♥/♥
Megan Fogarty 11 ♥/♥
Melissa Little 11 ♥
Meredith Logan 11 ♥, 12 ♥/♥
Miranda Burton 11 ♥
Natasha Norris 11 ♥, 14 ♥/♥
Rebecca Delgado-Corona 11 ♥, 13 ♥/♥
Stefanie Geilhart 11 ♥

2012
Ariel Tauro 12 ♥
Ashlee Base 12 ♥
Bridget Moore 12 ♥/♥
Carrie Bell 12 ♥/♥
Christi Allen 12 ♥, 14 ♥
Jenah Bellamy 12
Jennifer Mancini 12 ♥
Jessica Nielson 12 ♥, 13 ♥
Jessica Schulz 12 ♥/♥, 14 ♥
Julie Moore 12 ♥, 14 ♥

SURROGACY TOGETHER FRIENDS ASSOCIATION

Kim Narvasa 12 ♥, 13 ♥
Kristen Stepina 12 ♥/♥
Samantha Haberle 12
Stacy White 12 ♥
Tiffany Burke 12 ♥/♥
Tiffany Spring 12 ♥
Veronica Robison 12 ♥/♥
2013
Alexandra Meese 13 ♥/♥
Angela Donaldson 13 ♥
Amanda Dahmes 13 ♥
Amanda Lentz 13 ♥
Ashley Sefcik 13 ♥
Beth Watson 13 ♥, 14
Bobbie Pereira 13 ♥, 14 ♥
Britney Jenkins 13 ♥/♥
Candy Marden 13 ♥
Clara Cussen 13 ♥/♥
Jean Piepenburg 13 ♥
Jessica Makowski 13 ♥
Julie Calvello 13 ♥
Kayla McCullen 13 ♥
Kelly Murphy 13 ♥/♥
Kim Yancey 13 ♥, 14 ♥
Kristen Broome 13 ♥
Laura Theobald 13 ♥/♥
Lilianne Turk 13 ♥
Michelle Alexander 13 ♥/♥
Olivia Newsome 13
Paola Torres 13 ♥/♥
Renee Richards 13 ♥/♥
Roz Banks 13 ♥
Sara Schweikhart 13 ♥
Shannon Heacock 13 ♥
Tawna Krieble 13 ♥/♥
Tia Nielsen 13 ♥/♥, 14
Tina Valentine 13 ♥
2014
Andrea Shartzer 14 ♥
Basilia Sanchez 14

Brittany McGarity 14 ♥/♥
Brooke Bradley 14 ♥
Cecilia Blea 14 ♥/♥
Cristina Hernandez 14 ♥
Danielle Barrer 14 ♥/♥
Eva Calvillo 14 ♥/♥
Iris O'Grady 14
Jami Ward 14 ♥
Jennifer Armstrong 14 ♥/♥
Jennifer Weglarz 14 ♥/♥
Jade O'Connor 14
Josie Dahlager 14 ♥
Kasey James 14
Kate Mothershed 14 ♥
Katherine Estrada 14 ♥/♥
Lisa Norcross 14 ♥
Malia Scott 14
Megan Nielson 14 ♥
Michelle Anderson 14
Misty Campos 14 ♥
Robin Agnew 14 ♥
Roseli Cash 14
Savannah Boyer 14 ♥
Stacy Medich 14
Stephanie Provo 14
Suhaley Mitchell 14 ♥
Thealin Doung 14 ♥

INTENDED PARENTS
Carolyn Evans 07 ♥, 08 ♥
Celia Nolan 09 ♥, 10 ♥
Christy Deters 14 ♥
Daviv & Julia Ellis 13 ♥
Geoff Louvar & Hillary
Pearson-Louvar 11 ♥
George & Suzanne Sabo 13 ♥
Heather Bello 09 ♥, 13 ♥
Heather Chipain 12 ♥/♥
Joel & Laurie Mikuta 08 ♥
Jon & Christy Anderson 10 ♥
Katie Meyer 13 ♥/♥
Katie Susan 13 ♥
Larry & Robin Powell 13 ♥

Lars & Karen 08 ♥/♥
Laurie Mikuta 08
Leigh Elliott Mulready 10 ♥
Lyniel & Lauraleigh Weaver 11 ♥
Marc and Agnieszka Herman 14 ♥
Matthew & Jennifer Johnson 11 ♥
Rich & Wendy Anton 08 ♥
Samantha Meyer 13 ♥
Scott & Jessica Martin 11
Sten Holmstrom & Anders
Backlund 09 ♥/♥, 14 ♥
Stephanie Henry 08 ♥
Susan McGoldrick-Meerdink 08 ♥
Tonya McElroy 12 ♥

FRIENDS, FAMILY AND COMMUNITY

Alex, Kennidy, Ty, Tanner, Holden,
Madison Sierra
Allen & Jerry Day
Andy, Mikey, Ali Kirkbride
Brandon, Alex, Cameron Trammel
Breanna Benavides
Brian Baker, Derek & Ashley Lloyd
Carolyn Gravelle
Chad, Kaylie, Eli, Gabe White
Chris, Abigail, Caroline, Lillian, Juliet Weglarz
Chris & Jack Williams
Christina Escajeda
Claire Rotenberger
Courtney Billings
Danny, Emma, Lexi Norris
Danny, Sienna, McKenna, Gentry Mullins
Dave & Mardelle Anderson
Dave & Wendy Osborne
David & Lisa McElley
Eric, Ethan, Peyton Farley
Evan, Ethan, Juliana, Colin Bartlett
Gary, Samantha, Sydnie, Braeden Stern
Giogio Severi
Greg, Samantha, Ariel, Alexya Lund
Harold & Deshawn Valentine
Israel, Fernando, Jeniffer Torres
J. Alvarez & William Alvarez
Jeff Crockett
Jeremy, Blake, Christopher, Elizabeth,
Jessica Woolard

Jerimy, Dylan, Brianna Eaker
Jessica Hartman
Jodee Wilson
Joel, Matt, Bethani, Noah Legard
John, Jeremy, Tristan, Jessica Reeder
John, Jordyn, Bryant Thursby
Jon, Eli, Rolinda, Josh, Ryan Marden
Jonathan, Dominic, Danielle, Brian,
Mackenzie, James Arnold
Jonathon, Kadin, Elizabeth,
Allison Spring
Joyce, Chase, Emily Ferrell
Kenneth & Kent Hills
Kevin Blankemeier & Carrington
Tedford-Donahue
Kirk, Korbyn, Jaxyn, Preslie Logan
Linda Caldwell
Marge Barboza
Marissa Gerking
Mark, Maddie, Anthony, Jacob Turk
Michael, Natalie, Connor Lentz
Mike, Tony, Cade, Nina Menozi
Nic & Sarah Billings
Nick, Bailey, Trystan Uphoff
Nick, Olivia, Ryan, Nick Wheeler
Pat, Ashley, Anna, Abigail,
Adam Gerber
Patrick, Lia, Wes Murphy
Phillip Whiteman
Randy, Zach, Liam, Shane Jensen
Richard Nielsen
Rick & Ann Nielsen
Shayne, Joshua, Nicole,
Aiden Sokolowski
Skylar & Ethan Batdorf
Tom, Alexandria, Kailee, Aiden Puzzo
Travis & Bradley Booker
Tyson, Brittany, Katy Subia
Wes, Lexi, Kalvin Clemens

Surrogacy Together was established in 2013 as a way to join together in meaningful and engaging ways to give back and be advocates for Surrogacy.

Our founding Ambassadors and donors were there for us at the beginning to support and encourage the growth of our organization.

They have shared their great personal Surrogacy stories and made financial contributions that have allowed us to help create new families. We are incredibly grateful to this group, the backbone of our organization, for their efforts and resolute commitment to the Surrogacy Community.

Ambassadors

April Batdorf
Angela Simpson
Carolee Legard
Cathleen Hachey
Elizabeth Ziff
Erica Upoff
Gina Farley
Heather Fox Cote
Jennifer Taylor
Jill Reeder
Jodi Clemens
Kat Kirkbride
Kristen Broome
Kristle Menozi
Meredith Logan
Nic Billings
Paulina Lugo
Sarah Billings
Susan McGoldrick-Meerdink

Suzi Sabo
Tia Marie Nielson
Traci Woolard
Wendy Anton

Surrogacy Together Donors

Expect Miracles Surrogacy
Kumar Family Foundation
The Fertility Law Firm
Allison-McCloskey Escrow Company
Northridge Plaza Pharmacy
New Jersey IVF
Lorena Orozco
Amy Brooker
Marian Ceaser
Brent Cotman
Maureen Hawkinson
Carolee Legard
Meredith Logan
Cathleen Hachey
Natalie Parkin
Dana Mathews
Rhonda J Wile
Dave Anderson
Sandrealee Swaby-Perez
Heather Chipain
Stacie Grebner
Heidi Alderete
Susan McGoldrick-Meerdink
Betty Farnsworth
Jenna Slavin
Susanna Kapourales
Faith Livingston
Kimberly Eaker
Tracey Miller

Kristen Oconnell
Lena Corrado
Tracy Chizik
Mandi Montalvo
Elizabeth Borgen
Mehdi Lisi
James Fleming
Miatta Korpo
Jennifer Rickard
Yesenia Challenge
Jill Reeder
Iliana Lopez
Jodi Clemens
Patrick Shalvoy
Kristle Menozi
Carol Giorgio
Ndeye Seck
Cecilia Aguiar
Nic Billings
Sarah Billings
Cynthia Gutenplan
David Oconnell
Tia Nielsen
Elizabeth Ziff
Jackie Lufter
Janie Foley
Lori Flanders
Janno Heck
April Batdorf
Jasen Smith
Christine Gilbert
Jennifer Frazier
Courtneylee Martinez
Jennifer Tipton-Arnold
Cynthia Begley

Kirsten Ditkoff
Gina Farley
Laura Aniciet Wheeler
Jennifer Taylor
Lisa McElley
Kate Gerdes
Lorena Brenner
Katherine Hirschman
Massimo Scoppa
Michele Subia
Ted VanAcker
Paulina Lugo
William Myers
Phillip Whiteman
Aleyda Edmondson
Shelley Atwell
Jessica Hartman
Tammi Jensen
Lilianne Turk
Traci Woolard
Maribel Amador
Claire Rotenberger
Kathy Powers
Jamie Engleman
Linda Caldwell
Jamie-Lynn Rowan
Kat Kirkbride
Jennifer Daniel
Mardelle Anderson
Todd Crutchfield
Agata Brown
Signi Lisi
Christy Anderson
Natasha Norris
Carmela Cancino

About the
Author

Crystal Falk is a children's book author, product designer and mother of two beautiful children. Her passion is developing projects and products specifically for the surrogacy community and useful for pregnant women in general. In 2012, she became a surrogate for a wonderful family and had her first surrobaby in March 2013. In 2014, she started Birth, Bump and Beyond, LLC

When she is not creating new products, she is chasing her 4 and 2 year olds around the house and spending time with her fiancé. You can visit her at www.BirthBumpandBeyond.com/

About
Surrogacy Together

Our Mission is to share inspiring stories about the Surrogacy community with the world.

surrogacy gave me a chance at LIFE

We will educate and advocate for Surrogacy by sharing our uplifting, compelling, and empowering personal stories. We will share stories about our successful Surrogacy journeys and our happiest moments. We will create a visual story through our Photo Campaign sharing "What Surrogacy Means to Me" with the world. We will host events to educate future Intended Parents and Surrogates about the process and how to get started. We will provide financial grants to individuals and couples that otherwise would not be able to move forward with Surrogacy. We will host annual Celebrations to share our joy with everyone that has helped us Co-Create our "Families through teamwork."

WWW.SURROGACYTOGETHER.COM

If you are interested in finding out more information about surrogacy go to www.BecomeASurrogateToday.com

Made in the USA
San Bernardino, CA
26 August 2018